Dedicated to all
Troopers, their children,
and their families.

Be safe always.

My Aunt is a State Trooper, so what exactly does she do?

TROOPER

She helps people
all around,

People just like me and you!

Sometimes in
the morning,

And sometimes
in the night...

My Aunt
goes to
work to
make sure
everything
is alright

Some days she is on the highway, watching cars driving past,
1 Mile
Exit
8A

2 Mi
And she may have to pull over the ones that are going way too fast!
SPEED LIMIT 55
SPEED LIMIT 55
ABC·123
POLICE
POLICE

Other days she answers calls, there are so many things for her to do...

Lots of times she gets to
work with other heroes too!

Troopers are all over the nation

And although their uniforms
may not look the same...

They all serve to
protect the public,

and they all share
the Trooper name!

USA
Trooper
Protect & Serve
1234

Lots of other kids are just as lucky as me,

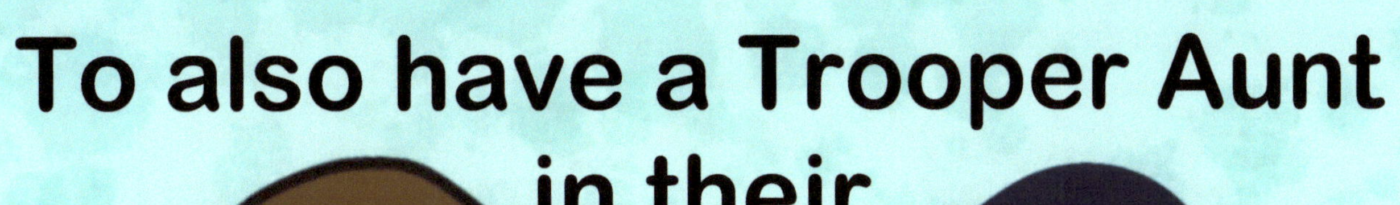

To also have a Trooper Aunt in their family!

You may see
Troopers in
cars, trucks,
motorcycles,
or boats
TROOPER
TROOPER

There are so many different transportation sources...
TROOPER

Troopers may also
fly in a helicopter,

and you may even see
some riding horses!

My Trooper Aunt is like a
super hero, she is brave
and she is strong

She is always
putting others
first while
working
all day and
all night long

Sometimes my Aunt
can't be here to play

But it's
because she is
working, and
helping
save the day!

My Aunt would love to be together all the time,

But it's hard for her to do
when she's out there
fighting crime

Whenever my Aunt is working,
there's one thing I know for sure

She loves me very much, and
I love her even more!

Sometimes when I get in bed
once the day is through,

I fall asleep and dream
that one day I'll be a
State Trooper too!

My Aunt is my hero, each
and every day...

I love my State Trooper Aunt
in every single way.